GW01376993

McDonagh, Bernard
Turkish village.
1. Turkey–Social life and customs–
Juvenile literature
I. Title II. Matthews, Jenny
956.1'038 DR432

ISBN 0–7136–2923–1

A & C Black (Publishers) Limited
35 Bedford Row, London WC1R 4JH

For my godson, Gustav Helmers

Acknowledgements

The author and publisher would like to thank the Küçükkurt and Serbest families, the Press Department of the Turkish Embassy in London, and the General Directorate of Press and Information, Ankara, for their help and co-operation.

The map is by Tony Garrett

Filmset by August Filmsetting, Haydock, St Helens
Printed in Hong Kong by Dai Nippon Printing Co. Ltd

Turkish Village

Bernard McDonagh

Photographs by Jenny Matthews

A & C Black · London

My name is Mustafa Kükçükkurt (you say Kuch-you-kurt). I am twelve years old and I live in Çandir, a village in the south of Turkey. My house is just outside the village, on the road to the Taurus mountains.

BULGARIA
GREECE
BLACK SEA
USSR
TURKEY
Istanbul
Bursa
Eskisehir
Ankara
Izmir
Antalya
Fethiye
Alanya
Adana
TAURUS MOUNTAINS
RHODES
CRETE
MEDITERRANEAN SEA
CYPRUS
SYRIA
0 50 100 150 km
N
main railways
main roads

Çandir is quite small – only a thousand people live in the village, most of them are farmers. My mum works at home and my dad has a shoe shop in Serik, our nearest town, which is about eight kilometres away. The nearest city is Antalya, which is forty kilometres away.

I have two older brothers, Kadir and Mehmet. Kadir is studying maths at university so he doesn't live at home. Mehmet is at High School in Çandir. He likes animals and he wants to be a vet.

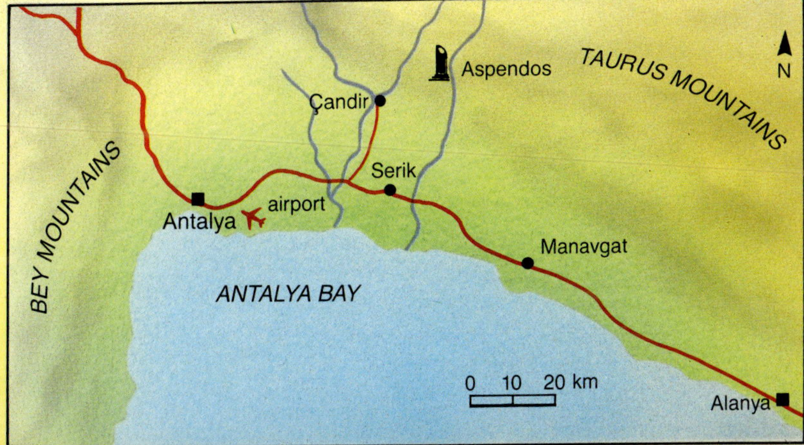

Until last year, I went to school in Çandir, but now I go to the Atatürk Middle School in Antalya. My mum and dad decided to send me here because they thought I would get better exam results.

There are about 800 children at my school. I'm a weekly boarder, which means I am here from Mondays to Fridays. I sleep in a hostel, ten minutes walk from school. At weekends I go home to Çandir or stay with my cousins in Antalya.

Lessons start at eight o'clock after our assembly. My best subjects are Turkish, English and maths. The English teacher asks lots of questions, but I don't mind that – I usually know the answers. I started learning English two years ago in Çandir. At first it was very hard, but now it's not so bad.

We have an hour's break for lunch then more lessons until three o'clock. Three times a week we have PE or volleyball. It helps if you are tall when you play volleyball – and I am not! But I still like playing, especially if my side is winning. Our teacher makes us work hard, even if it's very hot.

After school I do my homework. Then, if I have time, I play ping-pong with my friends. Sometimes I get permission from the hostel to go to the harbour. I like going down there to look at the boats. In summer there are lots of tourists in this part of Antalya. Sometimes I practise my English by talking to them.

I go home to Çandir about once a month, by minibus from Antalya. The bus is called a dolmush, and the Çandir dolmush belongs to the people of the village. It leaves Çandir every morning at eight o'clock, and comes back from Antalya at half past three.

The journey from Antalya to Çandir takes about forty minutes. Usually I find some friends on the bus who've come up to the city to shop. Then I can catch up with everything that's happened in the village since my last visit home. If there's nobody I know on the dolmush, I do my homework.

Çandir is six kilometres from the main road, between the Taurus mountains and the sea. The dolmush stops in the middle of the village near the shops and coffee houses, and I walk the last part of the way to my house.

It's good to meet people I know on the way home. Most of them are farmers, and all around there are fields of wheat, and olive trees, as well as peaches, figs and oranges and lemons. Often I'm lucky and I find Grandad out working on his land. He always asks me about school and what I've been doing in Antalya.

My dog Johnny seems to know when I am coming home. He rushes to meet me, barking and wagging his tail. He's always very glad to see me – I think he misses me a lot when I'm in Antalya.

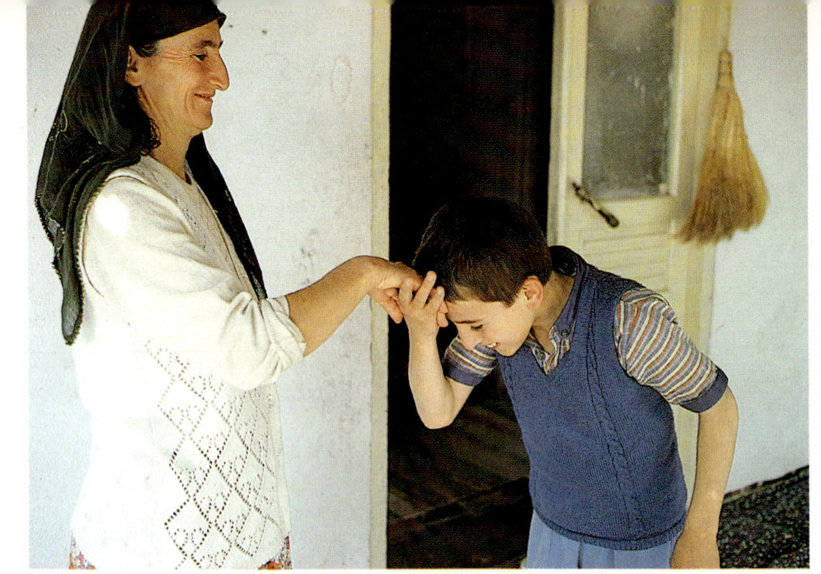

Of course, my mum is happy to see me, too. When I get to the house, she is waiting for me. I give her a special Turkish greeting. I put her hand first on my forehead and then to my lips. Then I find out if she is cooking something special for dinner.

When Mehmet comes home from school, we go to the greenhouse. We grow salad vegetables for the market in Antalya. There's always a lot to do in the greenhouse – the plants have to be sprayed and watered every day.

I help with picking the tomatoes and cucumbers and packing them in boxes for the market. Sometimes, when Mum isn't looking, I practise juggling with the cucumbers.

When we have finished in the greenhouse, I untie our cow and goat and drive them home. The goat is no problem, but the cow likes to stop and eat on the way. There's plenty of grass for her in our fields, but she always wants to try something different.

My mum is the only one who can milk the cow and goat. If Mehmet or I try to do it, they don't give much milk. I think that's because they know Mum best and are used to her hands.

While I'm waiting for supper, I do my homework. I have a lot, even at weekends. Sometimes Mehmet does his homework, too, or he helps me with mine.

Some evenings I help Mum make the supper. At least, I think it's helping – Mum says I'm a nuisance.

We're having beans tonight. All the vegetables we eat come from our garden or the greenhouse. That way we can be sure that they are fresh and really good. Our cow gives plenty of milk and we have eggs every day from our chickens, so Mum only needs to buy meat.

By the time my Dad gets home from Serik, supper is ready. We eat it in the living room, sitting on the floor. Mum puts down a large round piece of wood, then the table cloth, and on it she puts a tray loaded with food.

Mum usually cooks something special when I come home from Antalya. We start with soup, and today we're having lamb, with beans, potatoes, rice and salad. We always have home-made yogurt to eat with the food. Afterwards we have fruit, then tea. Turkish tea is weak and black, and I have mine with lots of sugar. If I am being very good, I help with the washing up afterwards.

Mum works very hard, so in the evenings I sometimes give her a massage. I walk very gently over a cushion on her legs and feet. This soothes them, while she leans back and relaxes.

My best friend, Ozcan, often comes round, or I go and see him. Tonight Ozcan has brought round some photographs of the party he had last month. The party was for his Sünnet. Every boy celebrates his Sünnet when he is about ten, to show that he is becoming a man.

After prayers in the mosque, Ozcan got on a horse and his dad led him in a procession around the village. People gave Ozcan presents and pinned money to his jacket. One of his photographs shows him wearing his special Sünnet clothes and riding the horse.

Most evenings Mehmet, Ozcan and I watch TV. Dad likes to read the paper and do the crossword. Grandma and Grandad often come over to talk to Mum and Dad, or to watch TV with us. Grandad never misses 'Dallas' if he can help it. I prefer sport or funny programmes.

In the village, people go to bed early because they get up so early in the morning. When our visitors have gone, Mum makes our beds ready on the divans in the bedroom and living room. Our divans are very comfortable, much better than the beds at my school in Antalya, so very soon I am fast asleep.

On Saturdays I take the dolmush to Serik and go to my dad's shop. Serik is on the main road. It's a busy town with lots of good shops.

Dad's shop is in the middle of town. He always has a lot of work to do. Just recently he got an apprentice called Adam to help him. Dad says Adam has learned the work quickly. I think my dad is a good teacher.

I don't know what I want to do when I grow up, but I don't want to be a shoemaker. When people come to buy shoes they take ages to make up their minds. Then when Dad tells them the price, they want to bargain with him. Sometimes people stay an hour in the shop, then go away without buying anything. But Dad doesn't mind that – it's the custom in Turkey.

Dad finishes work at about six o'clock. Some evenings he looks after our bees. He's a very keen beekeeper and has a book which tells him all about them. I think bees are interesting but I don't like them much. If they get angry they sting you.

The bees make honey which they store in wooden frames in the hive. Dad takes some of these frames out of the hive, but he leaves a few for the bees otherwise they would die of hunger. I like eating honey, and Mum says it's good for me.

Some days I like to go out and help Mum and my grandparents on the land. It's harvest time at the moment, so everyone is out cutting the wheat.

Grandad cuts his wheat by hand with a curved tool called a sickle. Grandma gathers the wheat into large bundles called sheaves, which she leaves in the sun for a few days to make sure the wheat is completely dry. That doesn't take long in summer because the sun is so hot.

We use a machine to cut the wheat in our fields. It's very powerful and it can do the job quickly.

Mehmet likes looking after Dad's car. He washes it every week, and checks the battery and the oil. I don't know much about cars so I'd rather let Mehmet do the work while I sit and talk to Grandad. He tells me all the news about Çandir, and I tell him what is happening in Antalya.

Grandad knows everyone in Çandir. He likes going to one of the coffee houses in the village to talk to his friends.

There are four coffee houses in Çandir. The men of the village meet in them to drink tea and play backgammon. In the evenings there are videos, usually of funny films. If there is an important football match on TV, the cafes are packed full.

In summer we usually go somewhere interesting in the car on Sundays. There are lots of good places to go to near the village – my favourite is the Roman theatre at Aspendos. It's outdoors, and there are enough seats for 30,000 people in the theatre. Mehmet says that, in Roman times, the theatre was used for plays and for fights between men and wild animals.

I like to climb to the top row of seats in the theatre and pretend that I can fly like Superman.

In the summer, it gets very hot in Çandir – sometimes the thermometer at our house even reaches 40° C. When the weather is like that, Ozcan and I try to persuade our parents to take us to the beach. The sea is only seven kilometres from Çandir, it's not far to go.

One the way home, our favourite treat is to stop off at a cafe and have some ice-cream. I like chocolate best, and Ozcan likes vanilla, so we have a mixture when we share an ice-cream. Dad doesn't eat ice-cream. He has a drink of ayran which is like runny yogurt.

Ozcan has an older brother whose name is Mehmet, the same as my brother. So that people can tell them apart, Ozcan's brother is called Mehmetçik, which means 'little Mehmet', because he wasn't very tall when he was younger.

Mehmet and Mehmetçik usually practise their dancing in Mehmetçik's garden. One of their school friends plays a sort of guitar called a sas for them to dance to.

Ozcan and I get bored watching our brothers dancing. There are some trees with big peaches in Ozcan's garden and when they are ripe, we go and pick them. Most of them are packed to go to the market in Antalya, but Ozcan and I still eat quite a lot.

Mehmet and Mehmetçik are folk dancers. At the moment, they spend every spare minute practising their dancing for the Youth Festival. They wear traditional clothes – baggy trousers called shalvar. Grandad says that in the old days, everybody used to wear clothes like these.

Lots of village people still wear shalvar because they are so comfortable in hot weather. I wear them sometimes.

Last May 19th, as a special treat, Dad took me to the Youth Festival. The festival is held on Atatürk's bithday, so that we remember his life, and that he was the great leader of modern Turkey. It's celebrated every year all over Turkey. In Antalya, it's held at the big football stadium.

Dad came to Antalya to pick me up from school. First we went to the statue of Atatürk, in the middle of the city. We watched young people lay flowers by the statue, then march to the stadium with bands playing all the way.

The stadium was packed full of people. The Governor of Antalya made a speech, and then the festival began. Boys and girls from every school in Antalya took part, starting with gym displays to music.

All of the teams were very good – but I think the best one was the one from my school. After the gym displays there was folk dancing. This was very exciting, but I think that Mehmet and Mehmetçik and their friends in Çandir can dance better.

Dad liked the part when the children on the opposite stand held up cards to make pictures. The nicest picture was the one showing the sun. This is the symbol of Antalya.

After the display was finished, Dad and I went to the city park for a walk. On the way there we found a man holding a huge balloon. He said it was to celebrate the Antalya football team, because they had just won the league championship. The man let me hold it for a bit while Dad took my picture. Ozcan and Mehmetçik should have seen that! They're really keen football fans.

After that we went to the zoo, and then the funfair. Dad gave me some money, and I had three rides on the dodgems. I wanted Dad to come with me, but he said he was too big. Maybe he was afraid that I would be a better driver than he is. Anyway, it was a very good ending to a day which I'll remember for a long time.